Praise for *Chiaroscuro Kisses*

The poems of G.L. Morrison's *Chiaroscuro Kisses* are alive with passion. Her lines are delicately crafted, evoking images so sharply etched you feel their edges on your skin. From the mythology of Daedalus, one of the 'architects of pleasure,' to the insistent aura of a departed lover, Morrison speaks from a depth that shocks each piece into life. The stanza of one poem, "Just Stop," ends "let everyone be quiet enough / to hear what the deluge has to say." Not an unreasonable request for Morrison's amazing work.

           Jewelle Gomez, *The Gilda Stories*

"The night forgives nothing, and there is nothing to forgive," G.L. Morrison writes in this empathetic and historically engaged collection. From a female psyche that reckons with the physical and metaphysical world, these poems achieve the seeing that comes with compassion. Like any good love story, the relationship of poet and subject in *Chiaroscuro Kisses* is one of complete attention.

  Dorianne Laux, *The Book of Men* and *Facts About The Moon*

What strikes me about these poems is their use of light. The candlelight that is "in love with your face," the light that "glittered off our arms like glass," and the morning light that witnessed Matthew Shepard's murder and "didn't recognize what it had done the night before." G.L. Morrison displays an immense range of emotions here. These are illuminating poems.

  Lesléa Newman, *October Mourning: A Song for Matthew Shepard*

Reading *Chiaroscuro Kisses* by G.L. Morrison took me to the numerous places in nature I call home. She understands the scent and feel of all things wild. Her words wrap around one's soul like a wild honeysuckle vine. Morrison's intensity of feelings toward women isn't written in word-search style. Emotions are laid bare for the reader to absorb and lose the self in each raw emotion-filled line.

           Judith K. Witherow, *All Things Wild*

If love had a voice, this would be it, speaking to us in *Chiaroscuro Kisses*. G.L. Morrison elevates language off the page, bringing us with her - whether it is into her passion for a particular lover, an insight into the dreams of houses, or writing from the perspective of love. G.L. Morrison is an important queer voice, and she is a unique voice. Read this book. Buy it for someone you love.

Janet Mason, *Tea Leaves*

In *Chiaroscuro Kisses*, G.L. Morrison confesses, howls, loves, remembers, and questions. In *Chiaroscuro Kisses,* Morrison writes, "I love poets who don't love me back," but she better prepare herself: readers of *Chiaroscuro Kisses* are certain to love her—and this book—back, with all the fierceness she desires. *Chiaroscuro Kisses* is a wonderful collection highlighting Morrison's lyricism and keen eye for imagery.

Julie R. Enszer, *Handmade Love* and *Sisterhood*

Chiaroscuro Kisses lives up to its name, as G.L. Morrison deftly guides us in and out of both light and shadowy places. Her poetic vision is superlative. There is something to admire in each and every poem, but the woman-to-woman love poems are some of the most poignant I've ever read. This is a collection to establish G.L. as a poet to be reckoned with. Buy this book - live with it - cherish it - and give G.L. lots of chiaroscuro kisses for creating it.

Chocolate Waters, *Charting New Waters* and *Take Me Like A Photograph*

G.L. Morrison's luscious poetic voice mates metaphors of intense originality and flavor with a formidable, brilliant queer intellect. Here is no mere ornamentation, but the piercing lyricism of a woman who actually has something to say.

Jan Steckel, *The Horizontal Poet*

G.L. Morrison's *Chiaroscuro Kisses* is a delight of investigation into all the rumors of women's emotions. But that's not all! This work ranges through folklore, history, geography – illuminating shadows, giving shade to the parched foothills of our last fifty years. Morrison asks "who knew we would survive?" With this language, this art, how could we not? Sometimes poetry is more useful than tourniquets. Get this book and add it to your own first-aid kit.

Elana Dykewomon, *Risk* and *Beyond the Pale*

Chiaroscuro Kisses skillfully straddles political fervor and desire with grace and empathy, bursting with color and precise detail. "Tiger" is a literary opus, a heartbreaking and raw lyric that seethes with an eloquence that can only be born of ferocious loss. Morrison has written one of the most inspiring collections of poetry I've seen in the last decade. It's the kind of work that 'slams' on the page, full of heart and courage.

Regie Cabico, *Flicker and Spark: A Contemporary Queer Anthology of Spoken Word and Poetry*

"Chiaroscuro," in terms of the visual arts: the inseparability of light and dark. "Chiaroscuro Kisses," in G.L. Morrison's eloquent and finely-crafted poems: the Yin and the Yang of love and loss, where nothing exists without its opposite. Light illuminates; light pins its victim on the fence. Night forgives nothing; there is nothing to forgive. These lyrical poems of witness, both personal and political, take my breath away as they will yours, and take their place among the most beautiful, the most powerful love poems ever written.

Ingrid Wendt, *Evensong*

CHIAROSCURO KISSES

G.L. Morrison

HEADMISTRESS PRESS

Copyright © 2013 by G.L. Morrison
All rights reserved.

ISBN-13: 978-0615875354
ISBN-10: 0615875351

This book may not be reproduced, in whole or in part, including illustrations, in any form (beyond that permitted by Sections 107 and 108 of the U.S. Copyright Law and except by reviewers for the public press), without written permission from the publishers.

Cover Art © 2009 and 2013 Jen P. Harris. The cover is a collage of two works by Jen P. Harris: *Untitled (American Kiss 9)*, ink on paper, 12 x 13 inches, from the multi-year project *American Kiss* (2009-2011); and detail from *Page*, ink, gouache on paper, 26 x 20 inches (2013). More images at jenpharris.com

Cover & book design by Mary Meriam.

PUBLISHER
Headmistress Press
60 Shipview Lane
Sequim, WA 98382
Telephone: 917-428-8312
Email: headmistresspress@gmail.com
Website: headmistresspress.blogspot.com

to my fangirls, my muses, the women who kiss and inspire me
- my strawberry girl, Angelique Hora
- my sweet kitten, Teresa Kennedy
- my beloved blasphemy, Salomé

Contents

Chiaroscuro	1
Now and What's to Come	2
Two Gentile Women	3
Hate Crime, Oct. 1998	5
Do Houses Dream	6
Wingless	7
Baba Yaga	8
Hump Day	9
Love's Perspective (We Are Like Bugs)	10
On Her Leaving	11
For You I Would	12
Relentless Blue	14
Borrowed from Candlelight	16
Haiku	17
Tiger	18
Just Stop	19
Traveling With Poets	21
Another Howl	23
Confession	25
Acknowledgments	28
Notes	29
About the Author	29

Chiaroscuro

In every first kiss
is the taste of the last.
A moon cut into slivers,
waning, until one night
the empty sky is
dark without her.

Now and What's to Come

Clouds spill in the night's sky
like milk in coffee
stirred by a white moon.
The scent of now
and what's to come
howls through the trees.
Here there is a smell of pine,
of paperclips, of morning coffees,
of reconciliations and recriminations,
of youth and cilantro.
The night forgives nothing
and there is nothing to forgive.
Tomorrow piggybacks
on the low clouds like rain.

Two Gentile Women Make Love after Reading that Orthodox Rabbis have Petitioned to Exclude any Mention of Gay and Lesbian Victims from a Holocaust Museum

This is what has happened and what has never happened.
I've heard it said there is a moment
—*There! No, there! Don't close your eyes
or you'll miss it!*—

in which the flesh of two become one flesh
a moment in which the body forgets itself,
joined and joining can no longer remember
which of the arms and legs it came in with.
This has never happened.

What has happened: When two stay two
and are the same or different.
We are wet with the scent of salt,
I am salt and you are salt

and we hold each other together with wet palms
the way sand sculptures are held together;

you hold me, keep my shape,
keep me from spilling out into you,
molecules akimbo.

I taste a bitterness on your skin
that is sweet to us.

I remember the Passover I spent with a friend
who was learning his Jewishness from a book,
whose parents had forgotten
their name, their grandparents' religion

the way they say the body forgets,
the way it doesn't forget.

There was something bitter to eat.
This is to remember.
This is to remember what others suffered to come here,
to survive, to make a place for us to survive in.

*When you think of us do you remember
the bitterness? How sweet it is to us.*

Your skin feeds me the memory of starving centuries.
Your fingers are the promise.
Your navel is a cup the angel drinks from.
Never forget.

Hate Crime, Oct. 1998

For Matthew Shepard

The light figures into everything. The cold indoor light
that diffuses the room with angles of distance and subterfuge,
and belief; the willing belief; the willingness to believe that one man
is like another, and the hand that two men extend to a third,
as they say "we're men like you, young like you, gay
like you, glad to have found you,"
is not the hand that will close into a fist
is not the hand that will close around his throat
holding the throat like a bottleneck, like an hourglass
that breath slips through like sand, until it stops.
Time has run out.
Whatever light there was figures into the moment.
The headlights of the blood-splattered truck,
the light that pinned him against the fence,
is an accomplice. The light that deliberated on the scene;
the weight of cold air, solitude, intolerant gravity,
the angle of resignation; none is innocent.

The morning light which didn't recognize what it had done
the night before, didn't recognize
what it found, wanted not to see him as a boy
tortured by other boys; as a man murdered for loving men
wanted to see him as the rags he had become
wanted to see him as a scarecrow left to frighten what?
to frighten who? out of these killing fields.

In the long night before day found him,
question and impatience talked in the dark.
The question of waiting met with the impatience of pain.
They talked about the angle
of history and the burden of coming snow.
Finally it was the light which came. The light which found him.
An arrangement of leaves conducted by brisk wind
updraft, downdraft, reason, unreason
all our lives blow down a street like this.

Do Houses Dream

Do houses dream?
Do the cupboards dream of chasing
broken dishes and lost teacups
and twitch like sleeping dogs?
Do they dream the cereal boxes full again?
Is that sometimes sound, the slow night-creaking
of walls, the house muttering in its sleep?
Does the house dream the kitchen full
of holiday relatives, traditional squabbles,
dry thinly carved regrets and football on TV after?
Does it people the rooms with whoever
lived here before us? Or has she forgotten them?
Will she forget us? The way we've forgotten before houses?
(Sometimes my hand goes out to flip a lightswitch
that isn't there, that never was.
I don't know what switch my hand remembers.)
Will she remember me that way? Will you?
Does it dream us fighting or making love,
of the things we've done or never would?
I can feel it cast the blue slope of our bodies
flickering like the shadow of the TV on the wall.
Beneath the carpet that knows the naked shuffle of our feet
and the floorboards which only know their weight
somewhere near the cracked foundation
is the heart of the house.
The multi-chambered heart of the house
unseen, rooms beneath rooms
that moles, last year's possum and some
sick stray cats come home to.
We don't know what's down here, dreaming.
There is a want that burrowed in.
There is a want grooved into the muscled heart
of the house like a warp in the floorboards
that unwary feet catch on.
The house has been dreaming us.
Shhh… don't wake it.

Wingless

Daedalus never understood the danger of joy.
He was imprisoned for this misunderstanding,
for making a device for the Queen's pleasure
when the King had ceased to please her.

The architects of pleasure are wingless
and short-sighted. The waxy geometry
of flight does not account for the angle
of wind against the skin or the sum

of sunlight. Logarithms of desire,
the delirious arithmetics of living,
dividing the sky between the sun
which will devour all our days

and the cold, blue sea. We fly akimbo
skimming the irreconcilable balance,
neither bird or fish enough to navigate
those distances. When I fall (and I will

fall) I know my father will fly on
without me. There are more sons
to be fathered on an unarrived shore.
Tomorrow is a margin in a ledger.

Baba Yaga

three times this house turned its back
to the sea and its door toward me
what choice did I have but enter

the hunger outburned any hope or risk
outweighed the distance
I came to know as regret

what choice did I have but lay
my chin on the shelf beside yours
filling the room with our far-flung bodies
stretched as deliberate as sleep

my memory of our arms and legs open
fills the house—your head in the kitchen,
hands flung into closets, one foot in the garage,
the heel of the other furrowing the yard

these rooms could not contain what we filled them with
and seemed to grow smaller around us
my house is still filled with the sounds of our sleeping

this was Baba Yaga's dream: that I was a hunger
you could never satisfy and not the woman
who followed the top she sent spinning
into forests, toward other houses

the truth is you were that hunger I fed myself to
until not even bones remained
and so had nothing left of myself for you

Hump Day

Thursday arrives in a gray pinstripe suit
he is all business
denies the rumor of the impending weekend
the possible merger of lovers
(and would-be lovers)

Thursday delivers the mail
with his accountant face
his eyes are the color of numbers
(the exact shade of 366)
his mouth is pursed like a decimal point
he wants a report, an accounting of my progress
(I am on the phone to next week
and pretend not to hear)
what is invested, what is gained, charts and graphs
a finger tap, tap, tapped on the bottom line
in the same rhythm as blood rushes
through my heart

I have no answer
(and only sometimes understand the question)

Thursday arrives in a gray pinstripe suit
he is all business
in his pocket is the thought of you, like a postcard
he delivers it to me
efficiently

the postcard says "I am beautiful, wish you were here."

Love's Perspective (We Are Like Bugs)

We are like bugs who live only a season.
This grass which has been green my whole life
will stay green. Green is all grass is.
The tree must be older than the dirt
which is forever kicked this way
and that; even beetles track or burrow,
push the dirt along.
The tree is a monument to its own immutability.
What could move it?

Stars are young as bottleflies.
They go out every time I close my eyes.
They were born with and will die with me.
Who's to say they won't?
You have to take their textbook word that
mountains remember a million years.
I've only known them for thirty.
Although Grandma's always known them,
and she's almost a million years old,
she's been wrong about so many things before.

What does it mean to say forever?
How long will I love you?
I am barely old enough to understand
the movement of trees.
If I could I would measure you
out behind me; let's not count by the days
that have yet to come.
I would love you a whole day in kindergarten.
I remember how long that was.

On Her Leaving

In the hallway where I had hung your picture
in my mind, there is something dense.
As if the air around united, heavy as honey,
gold as winter morning's light.
This is what is meant by the halos
in paintings; the holy manifest.
The split-tongued truth repeats itself,
weaves the moment thick with import;
you repeat yourself, insinuate
yourself into everything.
Now that you're leaving,
I see how the tenacious leaves
still hold enough color to attract the sun.
Their browning backs are veined
and simple as your small hands.

I am surrounded by this.
It appears as if by natural occurrence
inevitable, horrible, beautiful
as flood rain, tornadoes, erosion of cliff faces.
I am surrounded by this
honey-tongued, holy moment
in which love and leaving kiss.
In this instant, the moment (in which you were mine)
and the moment (in which you are not mine) are married.
This was true and this was never true.

I am surrounded by this: the weight
of wings, the distance of honey,
the taste of the word "tonight";
by measurement, by their scent and shades,
by the immutable geography
of smoke, of alarm clocks, of cotton,
of sex, of coffee cups, of calendars,
of tears, of wood and of stone.

For You I Would

If I could tear joy down from the walls
of the rooms it has slept in,
I would do it for you.
If I could peel the picture of you
off my eyes as if taking off a contact lens,
I would want you to wear it.

I would do it for your voice.
Your voice is like the smell of lemon-skins,
sweet-fleshed as blood oranges, light
as the blossoms of fruiting trees.
I would do anything for your voice.

Because for you
the night wraps her knee around the day.
For you, the day snuggles
sleepless, yellow in night's arms.
You are everything yellow.

You are the reason
school buses sprout like daffodils along the street.
Because of you, there is a middle light
in traffic columns; the yellow shriek
neither stop nor go, but hurry if you can
or BE AWARE stop is coming.
You are the submerged light that fingers us awake.
The light that filled the boat that we were fucking in
and glittered off of our arms like glass.

When you fly into my arms
you are a banshee, a broomstickless witch,
the kind of military plane that movies are made of—
rippling sex-charged metal and big guns.

When you laugh
with a laugh of banjos and possums

and weekends and stray cats
your laugh is blinding.
You bruise me with yellow laughter.

When you sing
you shake me into myself and away
from whoever I thought I was being.
What I find in the place
your singing travels to and stays,
I could not put in this verse.
There was no room.
A flying ocean, it swells
to fill all the space it enters.

I could die of how sweet you are; sweet and cold.
I could die of your autumned eyes. But
my death is in your feet, the end of everything,
the last rung in the ladder of your muscled calves,
rebelliously soft thighs.
I could die of your love; sweet and cold.
Sweeter than ice cream, sweeter than anything
my tongue has known.

If at night, wild and dim and alone,
I could press together the hot gray
that gathers above some buildings
we passed on our past-midnight walk
and tie it in a ribbon of its shadow
and its smoke and its thin yellow light
still pasted to some windows,
I would do it for you.

Relentless Blue

I look for you in this poem with both hands
every word like the fingers of a blind sculptor
searching for your familiar face in the sightless clay.

If I were a painter, what I want to say
to you would be a shade of blue that couldn't be bought
only blended by loving curiosity and relentless patience
blue as sun rising on the ocean after a storm

blue as dawn, obsidian about to shatter
in a wet cacophony of color.
Azure love. Sapphire uncertainty.
Hungers marbled turquoise and lapis lazuli.

If I were a sailor, this poem would be
a hundred days at sea.
Lips cracked with salt and silence.

Above me, in the wet, endless sky clouds row by
with a cargohold of storms and birds for barnacles.
Gulls shriek like lonely women.
Every star is an omen, I navigate by touch.

Below me, in the wet and endless sea
is everything I dare imagine, everything
that will ever and will never be
wide and spiny as puffer fish.

Infinitely blue and filled with stones, fish, and sunken
treasure; skeletons of clouds, birds, and stars;
sharks, mermaids, and the myriad of scuttling mysteries.
This poem is adrift in tomorrow's current
somewhere off the coast of yesterday.

Your hand on this page is bone china,
the pottery buried with Pharaohs, Klimt's

yellow kiss, swollen-mouthed as O'Keefe flowers.
Your hand on this page is the woman who waits
in a cottage overlooking the sea
where every hundred-day journey hopes to end.

Borrowed from Candlelight

Memorizing you, worshiping you,
the candles flicker on the table.
The light is in love with your face.

It glitters your cheek, strokes your neck,
filling the beads at your neck with suffused fire.
You are noosed in burning kisses.

The light is in love with your skin
and glints off the sweat of dancing,
like the light caresses the river.

I watch it make love to you.
Here the candlelight kisses the ring
in your nipple, kisses the puckered nipple.

I am entranced by this.
The light kisses me with the same mouth.
I taste its loving you.

Your mouth follows the path of the light toward this kiss.
You kiss me, holy me, honey me with soft fires.
Dancing, your navel purses and opens

its lips in imitation of kissing.
I memorize your lips, hips, eyes, navel and breasts,
holy honeyed light-filled breasts.

I memorize you tonight, borrow
enough of you from this candlelight
to fill another hundred poems.

Haiku

the storm raging inside
wets us both, turning you
the color of rain

Tiger

I dreamed in a language I no longer knew
upon waking. I dreamed that you wore me
like a tiger skin. That you walked the jungle
cities and looked at passersby through my eyes.
What they saw when they looked back
was not reflected in your iris or mine.
My name rode on the back of your neck
like god's on a homunculus. If the signature
itched, you could not reach (with my fingers)
to scratch it. West of Eden and still walking,
a Colossus kicking dirt clouds; the burden
of two feet in the same footprint.
Both exiles from paradise.
When my love and its expectations grew
heavy and ill-fitting, loose with rough walking,
you shrugged me off. I fell
in stripes but landed on all my feet,
gamboled away… and woke alone
and monolingual.

Just Stop

Stop in the middle
of what you were saying.
In the middle of what you were
doing, of what you were about to
do—just stop. Say, do, nothing.

For once let everyone everywhere stop.
Let there be just silence and intention.
Stop birds, band-leaders, lovers
and politicians. Undam the rivers
and let everyone be quiet enough
to hear what the deluge has to say.

Allow yourself to be quiet,
not misunderstood, for this is
an unmistakable silence,
a legendary pause.

Drop whatever you are holding,
whatever flag or grudge you hold dearest.
Unclench your fists. You will need
both hands empty to lift the silence.

Stop your watch, phone, clock, war,
ads and promising. Stop waiting.
Stop time. Stop being afraid of death.

Stop mirrors. You don't need them.
You can't recognize yourself.
You only know you
for where you have to be next
and how late you may arrive.
Who knows how often
you've already passed yourself
in the street unrecognized?

Stop lying. Stop for one second.
Don't move your arms so much.
Let's meet in the sudden strangeness
of doing, saying, expecting nothing.

Put down your guns, maps, spreadsheets,
ghosts and indifference. Forget yourself.
You never knew her. In that second
of silence, with the whole world stopped
and empty, try and remember
—before it all starts again
before the noise of sheep, soldiers, police
sirens, athletes, mothers, trends and traditions
rips the green air—
if anything you dropped was worth
the weight of picking it up again.

Traveling With Poets

She autographed me "beautiful
co-surrealist" and reminded me
of the birthday I gifted us both
a klezmer band under the stars and she
gifted me with a re(intro)duction
to a punk rock ukulelist who wrote
poetry you could marry.

I wanted the Oregon Book Award
for her more than any nomination
I have skirted or coveted for myself.
If you knew the ferocity of my jealousy
you would know what this means.

Soon it begins to rain sheep
and other surrealist poets.
Where are we going with this?

Until Mike read a poem about
a friend's vacation, I forgot all
my waiting to reenter the country.
Off the ferry from Victoria
having learned the ident(if)ication
sufficient to get me into Canada
was not sufficient to get me out again.

   All
        day
                from
      one
queue
        to another
thinking my rage and entitlement
should be enough
to prove me an American.

Or on the way out of Nogales
armored only in white privilege
I pushed past a row of guards
with machine guns
to get the suitcases
they were not letting us take
off the train. Brown and white
rows of other luggage-hungry travelers
watch but do not join me.

*"I got in the habit of writing
poems about places I've never been,"*
the featured poet confessed
and the line I selected
from the fishbowl prompted *"Yes,
Paris, that's worth the price of maps."*

But Paris was a terrible judge of Beauty
and squandered Eris's apple
without taking a golden delicious bite
and Paris Syndrome is a sickness
of Japanese businessmen, a cultural flu
of disillusionment. *"They can fake
an out-of-body-experience."* But don't.

Is Dorianne home from Paris?
I can never forgive her
the fan who tattooed a line of poetry
on her back. I want this now more
than any Pulitzer or other book award.

Another Howl

I have howled at night alone
like a dog, hollow and wild
I have coo-whimpered
the dying song of a pigeon caught in the dog's mouth
my heart is a double-throated singer, duet of myself
killer-howl/killed-cry
I stalk myself through these mad streets where
passing cars toss their headlights in puddles like discarded cigarettes
cherry burning
their reflection set my feet on fire
acid clouds darken with chemical rain
my shadow splashed at the side of building
gray as Hiroshima ash

the best minds of my generation were destroyed by greed
and parents' dotage and I didn't see it
I was busy learning not to look, not look
starving in our mothers' kitchens
clothed only in our fathers' prejudices
starving, cynical, naked
we dragged ourselves through alleys and days
looking for nothing

anger is justice defiled
but we never knew her innocent
justice was turning tricks before we were born
we danced the faggot streets
knew everything, expected nothing
and were never surprised
burning adolescent tallow off our quick-lit wicks
saving nothing for tomorrow

who knew we would survive?

starry nights, so many starry nights
seen through madhouse windows

constellations sordid and stale
yesterday's failed suicide attempt
stars falling like accusations
beautiful in their falling
belle morte, beautiful little deaths
fireworks, light show, dying stars
beautiful, beautiful
the machinery of night
grinds on, gears slip
noticing us not at all

Confession

I can't help it. I'm addicted to them.
Confessional poets. Plath was my first.
I could taste her words. Her tongue
fluttering in my mouth like ravens,
dry lizard licks and teeth.
Her poetry said "I will fuck you
and I will fuck you up."
Her poetry said "I will love you without caring
whether you love me back."
But she lived like she cared.
She died without knowing how much I loved her.

I was eleven and had fucked a dozen girls before I knew
what I was, what fucking them made me.
I discovered myself a lesbian while watching the Miss America Pageant,
face glued to the screen, whispering encouragements and consolations
to my choices. I would go to sleep dreaming of Miss Alaska.
In my princess canopy bed we rubbed more than noses that night.

I watched myself watching TV that day
and asked myself what made it so intense, so important.
It was, even at eleven, a guilty pleasure,
this contest that reduced women to nothing more than their bodies
breasts and butts and big hair battling
for modeling contracts and fur coats
—prizes no self-respecting 70s woman would accept, even at 11.
My hungriest fantasies haven't changed in 30 years:
drowning in the soft luxury of women in fur.

What then about that technicolor moment sang
"there she is, she's a lesbian"
that hours of girl-grinding lips and hips had not?

I knew in that moment, torn between too much beauty
and not enough crowns to reward it,
that I loved women the way I loved books.

Ravenously, as fast and as many as I could lay my hands on.
Reading indiscriminately in every genre
and savoring my favorites again. Slowly.

I wanted to own that moment, those women,
to wrap that exact second in leather bindings
lined up on a shelf where I could take down
each pout, each whimper, bathing suit, flaming
baton, sequined gown, each breathless prom queen.
Whenever. I. Wanted.
I wanted to eat them like poetry.
I wanted to bite women
and spit fire. I wanted to hear their confessions.
I wanted to give them something to confess.

Flat as on a page, beauty queens on the TV screen
might have thrilled my preteen heart but poets stole my soul.
I have always loved confessional poets.
Poets who don't kiss. But tell anyway.
Poets who curdle soft words in hard mouths.
Poets who know love is a picnic on a battlefield,
where treaties are drawn beside lines in the sand
and a ceasefire is only long enough for "pass
the butter" and fucking women who don't kiss,
there's no time
to bother with pecks or smooches or kind words.

I confess I love poets who don't love me back.
I confess I love books who don't love me back.
I confess their indifference makes no dent in my titanium love.
I confess that I have used poetry
the way some men use women.
I confess that I have used poetry to capture lovers.
I confess that I have been used by poetry, captured by love.
I confess to loving confessional poetry and women I don't know
and to sometimes confusing the two.

I like kind women and unkind poets.
I like her mouth
even if she'll never kiss me.
I like her need, her sacred rage, her vision of heaven.
I like how she'll fuck me with a handful of well-lubricated words
in front of a crowd of drunken critics and other bankrupt poets.
Her poetry is a communion wafer forced onto the tongue.
This is my body. Don't forget it.
The saliva in her performance kiss is wine.
Since teeth come before tongue in her kisses,
there is blood in the wine.
You will remember her.
I worship her or her poem, it's the same.
I make a religion of loving confessional poets, old and new.

What strange angels they are: leading us into the purgatory
of masturbation and memory to find salvation, a well-placed caesura,
in the daily cadence of incest, abortion, divorce

and affairs illicit and ill-fated.
We confess not sins but survival. We refuse absolution.
Godless angels. Sullen saints. The truth does not free us.
Confession is its own reward.
O my sister confessors, my succubi,
mea culpa, mea culpa.

Acknowledgments

My thanks to the editors of the following publications, in which these poems first appeared, sometimes in slightly different versions:

Ghost Town Poetry: "Another Howl"

Manzanita Quarterly: "For You I Would" and "Two Gentile Women Make Love after Reading that Orthodox Rabbis have Petitioned to Exclude any Mention of Gay and Lesbian Victims from a Holocaust Museum"

Sixfold: "Wingless," "Baba Yaga," and "Relentless Blue"

Strophes: "Two Gentile Women Make Love after Reading that Orthodox Rabbis have Petitioned to Exclude any Mention of Gay and Lesbian Victims from a Holocaust Museum"

The Bridget Poems: "Hump Day" and "Borrowed from Candlelight"

Verseweaver: "Two Gentile Women Make Love after Reading that Orthodox Rabbis have Petitioned to Exclude any Mention of Gay and Lesbian Victims from a Holocaust Museum"

Yes is a Pleasant Country (CD): "Now and What's to Come"

NOTES

"Two Gentile Women Make Love after Reading that Orthodox Rabbis have Petitioned to Exclude any Mention of Gay and Lesbian Victims from a Holocaust Museum" won an award from the Oregon State Poetry Association.

"Hate Crime, Oct. 1998" is inspired by the life and death of Matthew Shepard, a young gay man who was tortured and murdered near Laramie, Wyoming in October 1998. This poem has been widely distributed at rallies and protests, and reprinted in many LGBT regional newspapers. It remains available, free and clear, for anyone to use in educating about, protesting, or preventing violence and hate crimes.

ABOUT THE AUTHOR

G.L. Morrison's nonfiction writing stands at the crossroads of racial/economic justice, body-hatred/fat-activism/slut-shaming, and LGBT representation/pop culture. She has received awards and publication in both the mainstream and the margins. Her poems and prose have appeared in *Evergreen Chronicles, Girlburn, Sinister Wisdom, We'Moon, Mother Jones, The Advocate, Manzanita Quarterly,* and in anthologies including *Best of Best Women's Erotica* (Cleis Press, 2005), *Mom: Candid Memoirs* (Alyson Books, 1998), *Pillow Talk II* (Alyson Books, 2000), and *How Can You Say We're Not Related* (Scurfpea Publishing, 2012). She is a blogger, teacher, survivor, artist, publisher, and editor.

Headmistress Press Books

Lovely - Lesléa Newman
Teeth & Teeth - Robin Reagler
How Distant the City - Freesia McKee
Shopgirls - Marissa Higgins
Riddle - Diane Fortney
When She Woke She Was an Open Field - Hilary Brown
God With Us - Amy Lauren
A Crown of Violets - Renée Vivien tr. Samantha Pious
Fireworks in the Graveyard - Joy Ladin
Social Dance - Carolyn Boll
The Force of Gratitude - Janice Gould
Spine - Sarah Caulfield
Diatribe from the Library - Farrell Greenwald Brenner
Blind Girl Grunt - Constance Merritt
Acid and Tender - Jen Rouse
Beautiful Machinery - Wendy DeGroat
Odd Mercy - Gail Thomas
The Great Scissor Hunt - Jessica K. Hylton
A Bracelet of Honeybees - Lynn Strongin
Whirlwind @ Lesbos - Risa Denenberg
The Body's Alphabet - Ann Tweedy
First name Barbie last name Doll - Maureen Bocka
Heaven to Me - Abe Louise Young
Sticky - Carter Steinmann
Tiger Laughs When You Push - Ruth Lehrer
Night Ringing - Laura Foley
Paper Cranes - Dinah Dietrich
On Loving a Saudi Girl - Carina Yun
The Burn Poems - Lynn Strongin
I Carry My Mother - Lesléa Newman
Distant Music - Joan Annsfire
The Awful Suicidal Swans - Flower Conroy
Joy Street - Laura Foley
Chiaroscuro Kisses - G.L. Morrison
The Lillian Trilogy - Mary Meriam
Lady of the Moon - Amy Lowell, Lillian Faderman, Mary Meriam
Irresistible Sonnets - ed. Mary Meriam
Lavender Review - ed. Mary Meriam

www.ingramcontent.com/pod-product-compliance
Lightning Source LLC
Chambersburg PA
CBHW070043070426
42449CB00012BA/3153